"Your imagination is everything. It i:
coming attractions." – Albert Einstein

Dedicated to Quinn and Owen (our Kate and Sam), who the book is based upon!

Stop Stealing My Imagination!

ISBN-13: 9798895901199

Illustrated by Quinn Pelletier

Kate was a little girl with a very big imagination. She had magical dolls that lived in a bouncy space station.

They flew around the galaxy rescuing stranded fairies on stars.

Then celebrated with ice cream at a carnival on Mars.

As Kate was playing in her room,
her older brother, Sam, came in and said,
"YOU can't live on Mars!
There's no oxygen and the planet is red!"

Kate said, “Fine, then they will live on Jupiter together!”
He responded, “No! Jupiter is full of ammonia
and has stormy weather.”

Kate whined, “But my dolls can use their magic wings to fly around!”

Sam stated, “That’s silly!

They aren’t alive and can’t get off the ground.”

You see, Sam had been learning a lot of facts at school.
And most of the time, Kate thought they were quite cool.

But today as she played in her world of pretend,

she decided that Sam's facts needed to end

and SCREAMED...

STOP STEALING My IMAGINATION!

They began to fight as siblings often do. Sam kept telling his facts and Kate cried that they weren't true.

Her dolls were magical and could really live in space.

He was stealing her imagination, and it put tears on her face.

Mom and dad came to her room and tried to stop the fight.

Both kids told their side and felt they were right!

Their parents smiled and gave each other a knowing look.

They asked the kids to sit down and pulled out a book.

It held stories Sam told them when he was Kate's age.

There must have been A LOT because words took up every page!

Mom read aloud his tales about a rainbow park with cotton candy.

It had fire trains on red tracks and the beaches were sandy.

Sam had an imaginary friend who was thousands of years old.

She fought ninjas and bad guys with a sword made of gold!

He also had a magical spaceship that he could fly, which would carry him to his big, red house in the sky.

The family laughed hard as they read every page,

because Sam's imagination was just as vivid at Kate's age.

He started to remember the colorful fire trains and cotton candy,

and the epic castles he built on the beaches that were sandy.

Sam felt proud he had a cool, ninja fighting friend and that he, too, used to play in a land of pretend.

When they were done reading, mom and dad looked at the kids and said, “imagination and knowledge can *both* live inside your head.”

“The world can be a magical place, and there is so much we don’t know. Without wondering what’s possible, our brains cannot grow!”

“If you blend what you learn through education, with all the possibilities of your imagination, you can become anything you put your mind to: an astronaut, a teacher, or a keeper at the zoo.”

“So, go have fun, play together, and wonder about the unknown, because before you know it, you will be fully grown.”

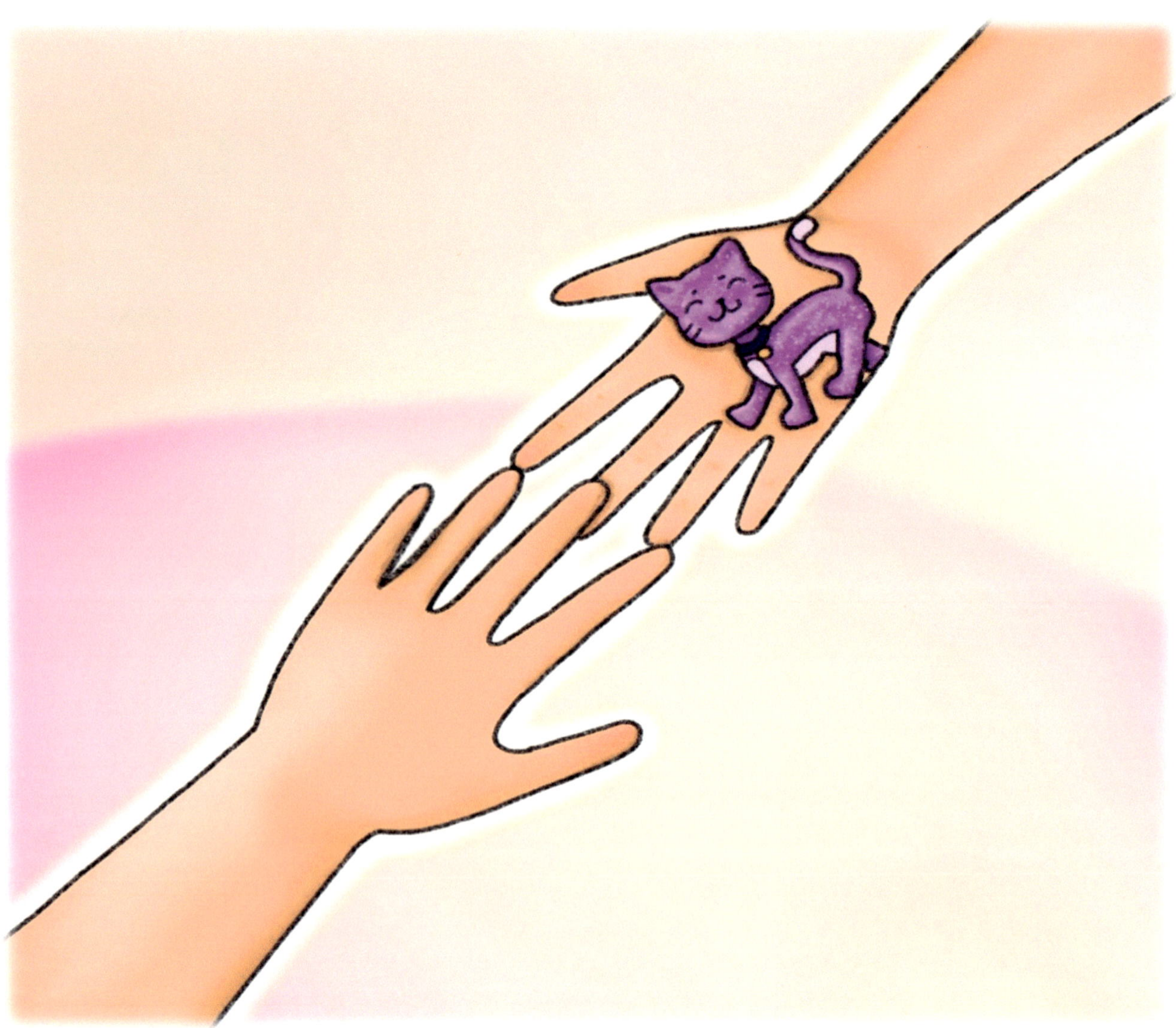

“There are plenty of activities for you both to enjoy.
Kate may even let you play with her magical toys!”

Kate smiled and said she wished she had a cool ninja fighting friend.

As they walked to his room, Sam explained why Mars is red.

Sam then asked Kate to describe her space station

and promised to stop stealing her imagination.

THE END

Made in United States
Troutdale, OR
11/24/2024